Dear Parent:

Remember the first time you read a book by yourself? I do.
I still remember the thrill of reading the words Little Bear said
to Mother Bear: "I have a new space helmet. I am going to
the moon."

Later when my daughter was
learning to read, her favorite I
Can Read books were the funny
ones—Danny playing with the
dinosaur he met at the museum
and Amelia Bedelia dressing
the chicken. And now as a new
teacher, she has joined the
thousands of teachers who use
I Can Read books in the classroom.

I'm delighted to share this commemorative edition with you.
This special volume includes the origin stories and early sketches
of many beloved I Can Read characters.

Here's to the next sixty years—and to all those beginning
readers who are about to embark on a lifetime of discovery that
starts with the magical words *"I can read!"*

Kate M. Jackson
Senior VP, Associate Publisher, Editor-in-Chief

I Can Read Book® is a trademark of HarperCollins Publishers.

The Berenstain Bears' New Pup
Copyright © 2005 by Berenstain Bears, Inc.
Illustration on page 1 copyright © 1963 by Fritz Siebel; renewed 1992 by the Estate of Fritz Siebel.
Additional illustrations on pages 36–39: Amelia Bedelia sketch copyright © 2013 by the Estate of Fritz Siebel from *Amelia Bedelia: Fiftieth Anniversary Edition*. Berenstain Bears sketch copyright © 2017 by Berenstain Bears, Inc. Biscuit sketch copyright © 2017 by Pat Schories. Danny and the Dinosaur sketch copyright © 2017 by Anti-Defamation League Foundation, Inc., The Author's Guild Foundation, Inc., ORT America, Inc., United Negro College Fund, Inc. Fancy Nancy sketch copyright © 2017 by Robin Preiss Glasser. Frog and Toad sketch copyright © 2017 by the Estate of Arnold Lobel. Little Critter sketch copyright © 2017 by Mercer Mayer. Pete the Cat sketch copyright © 2017 by James Dean. Pinkalicious sketch copyright © 2017 by Victoria Kann. All rights reserved. Manufactured in China. No part of this book may be used or reproduced in any manner whatsoever without written permission except in the case of brief quotations embodied in critical articles and reviews. For information address HarperCollins Children's Books, a division of HarperCollins Publishers, 195 Broadway, New York, NY 10007. www.icanread.com

Library of Congress Cataloging-in-Publication Data
Berenstain, Stan.
  The Berenstain Bears' new pup / Stan & Jan Berenstain.—1st ed.
    p. cm.—(An I can read book)
    p.   cm. — (An I can read book)
  Summary: Mama, Sister, and Brother are excited about the puppy they bring home from Farmer Ben's farm, even though she takes a lot of care.
  ISBN 978-0-06-257272-1
  [1. Pets—Fiction. 2. Dogs—Fiction. 3. Animals—Infancy—Fiction. 4. Responsibility—Fiction. 5. Bears—Fiction.] I. Berenstain, Jan. II. Title. III. Series.
PZ7.B4483Bffd 2005   2004006237
[E]—dc22
Typography by Scott Richards

16 17 18 19 20 SCP 10 9 8 7 6 5 4 3 2 1 ❖ First Edition

I Can Read!

BEGINNING 1 READING

The Berenstain Bears'
New Pup

Stan & Jan Berenstain

HARPER
An Imprint of HarperCollinsPublishers

One day Mama and the cubs
went to Farmer Ben's farm.
They went there to buy
some fresh eggs.

"Look!" said Brother. "There is a sign
on Farmer Ben's barn door."
The sign said PUPS FOR SALE!
"Hmm," said Mama.
"Farmer Ben's dog, Queenie,
must have had pups."

"Oh, Mama!" said Sister.

"May we have one? May we?

May we? Please?"

"We came to buy eggs," said Mama.

"Not a pup."

Farmer Ben was in the barn.

So was his dog, Queenie.

Queenie was in a box with her pups.

There were many pups.

Some of her pups were having lunch.

Some were sleeping.

One of them was playing
with a piece of straw.

"Oh," said Sister.
"I want that one!
He is so cute."

"That one is a she," said Farmer Ben.

"How can you tell?" asked Brother.

"There are ways," said Farmer Ben.

"Now, cubs," said Mama,
"buying eggs is one thing.
Buying a pup is quite another."

"Oh, Mama," said the cubs,

"may we have her?

May we? May we? Please?"

"A pup is not just something
you have," said Mama.
"A pup is something
you have to take care of."
"We will take care of her!"
said the cubs.

"A pup is something you have to clean up after," said Mama.
"We will clean up after her," said the cubs.

"A pup likes to get into things,"
said Mama.
"We will watch her every second!"
said the cubs.

Farmer Ben picked up the pup

that was playing with the straw.

He put her in Mama's hands.

The pup looked into Mama's eyes.

The pup licked Mama's nose.

The pup wagged her tail…

and Mama's heart melted!

On the way home,

they named the pup Little Lady.

They named her "little"

because she was little.

They named her "lady"

because she was a she.

"Yum!" said Papa Bear
when they got home.
"A dozen farm-fresh eggs!"
"And one farm-fresh pup!"
said Sister Bear.

Mama was right about Little Lady.

She did have to be cleaned up after.

She left a puddle in one corner…

and a calling card in another.

And she did like to get into things.

She got into Mama's baking flour.

Cough! Cough! Cough!

She got into Papa's fishing tackle.

What a tangle!

She got into Farmer Ben's
farm-fresh eggs.
What a mess!

"Hmm," said Mama.

"I am going back to Farmer Ben's."

"You're not going to take Little Lady back to Farmer Ben's?" cried Sister.

"No," said Mama.

"I am just going to get another dozen eggs."

"I can read! I can read! Where are the books for me?"

One question from a young reader sparked a reading revolution!

A conversation between the director of Harper's Department of Books for Boys and Girls, Ursula Nordstrom, and Boston Public Library's Virginia Haviland inspired the I Can Read book series. Haviland told Nordstrom that a young boy had burst into the children's reading room and asked her where he could find books that were just right for a brand-new reader like himself.

Determined to fill this gap, Nordstrom published *Little Bear* by Else Holmelund Minarik, with illustrations by Maurice Sendak, in the fall of 1957. The response was immediate. According to the *New York Times*, "One look at the illustrations and children will grab for it. A second look at the short, easy sentences, the repetition of words, and the beautiful type spacing, and children will know they can read it themselves."

Delightful and wonderfully warm, *Little Bear* served as the template for the series, and now, sixty years later, we have over four hundred I Can Read stories for our youngest and newest readers!

Where the Ideas for the Characters Came From

Berenstain Bears

Stan and Jan Berenstain were cartoonists in the 1950s. When their sons began to read, they submitted a story about a family of bears to author, editor, and publisher Ted Geisel (aka Dr. Seuss), which was published as *The Big Honey Hunt* in 1962. Geisel labeled their next effort "Another Adventure of the Berenstain Bears." That's how the bears got their name!

Biscuit

One day while watching her daughter play with their neighbor's frisky dog, Alyssa Capucilli was struck by her daughter's patience and gentle nature, as well as the fact that her little girl thought the dog understood every word she said. That was the inspiration for the little yellow puppy and his sweet companion. Pat Schories's warm illustrations capture their tender relationship.

Pete the Cat

When James Dean first saw Pete, he was a tiny black kitten in a shelter. Pete looked like he had been starved and his black fur was a mess. At first, James had no interest in Pete—black cats were bad luck, after all! But the scrawny little fellow stuck his paw out of the cage, wanting to play! James took Pete home. And even though James chose to paint Pete the Cat blue (his favorite color), James realizes now that black cats are actually very good luck.

Danny and the Dinosaur

In 1958, cartoonist Syd Hoff's daughter Susan was going through a rough surgery, and one day, Syd decided to draw a picture to cheer her up. It showed a dinosaur with Syd's brother on its back. When Susie saw the picture, she exclaimed, "Danny and the dinosaur!" and that night after the family went to bed, Syd wrote the story.

Pinkalicious

Victoria Kann's daughters could never seem to get enough of cupcakes or the color pink! One year, as an April Fools' joke, Victoria told her family and friends that one of her daughters had turned pink from eating too many pink cupcakes—and so the idea for *Pinkalicious* was born!

Frog and Toad

The characters of Frog and his best friend, Toad, might have been inspired by . . . a horror movie! Arnold Lobel and his daughter, Adrianne, went to see a movie called *Frogs* at the drive-in. However, the movie featured not frogs, but toads! Adrianne told her dad about the many differences between the two—and two years later the first Frog and Toad book, *Frog and Toad Are Friends*, appeared.

Little Critter

Mercer Mayer was doodling around one day in 1974 when he drew a shape like a gourd, put two eyes on it, scribbled a nose connecting the eyes, then got coffee and forgot about it! The next day, he noticed a small piece of paper on the floor. It was his gourd. He added fuzzy hair and a big mouth; short stubby arms and feet. Mercer had created a fuzzy little "woodchuck-y porcupine" thing that became Little Critter!

Fancy Nancy

When Jane O'Connor was a small girl, every Sunday, when her grandma and great aunts came to visit, Jane would greet them at the door in a tutu and a pair of her mom's high heels. She thought she looked très glamorous!

Years later, while she was fixing dinner one night, the name Fancy Nancy flew into Jane's head, and a star made her debut!

Amelia Bedelia

Amelia Bedelia was inspired by Peggy Parish's third-grade students at the Dalton School in New York City. The children mixed up words, and Parish found them hilarious. That gave Parish the idea for Amelia Bedelia—a character who takes every word literally and embraces life with an outlook that is forthright and optimistic. Illustrator Fritz Siebel worked with Parish to create the perfect look for the conscientious cleaning lady.

Early Character Development

The Berenstain Bears

Stan and Jan Berenstain's early sketches from *The Berenstain Bears Clean House*

Pete the Cat

James Dean's first painting of Pete the Cat

JAMES DEAN
12. 26. 99

Frog and Toad

Early character sketch of Frog and Toad

Biscuit

Biscuit character sketches

Pat Schories's early sketches from *Biscuit*

Pinkalicious

Victoria Kann's sketches for the picture book *Pinkalicious*

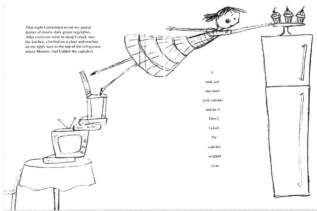

Amelia Bedelia

Fritz Siebel's sketches for the picture book *Amelia Bedelia*

Danny and the Dinosaur

Syd Hoff's early cover sketches for *Danny and the Dinosaur*

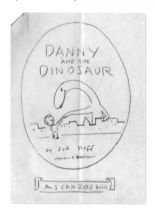

Little Critter

Mercer Mayer's early character sketches of Little Critter

Fancy Nancy

Robin Preiss Glasser's character sketches and cover sketch for *Fancy Nancy and the Boy from Paris*

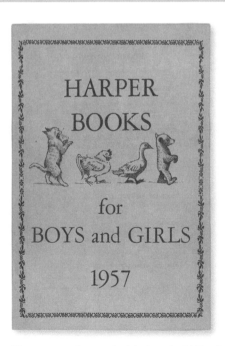

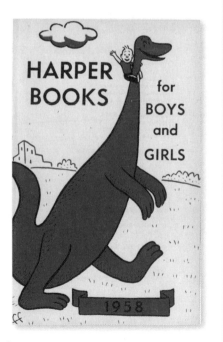

These two catalogs marked the launch of I Can Read!

Sixty Years of I CAN READ

1957
Little Bear

1958
Danny and the Dinosaur

1959
Sammy the Seal

Emmett's Pig

1960
Cat and Dog

1961
*Little Bear's Visit**

1963
Amelia Bedelia

1970
*Frog and Toad Are Friends**

A Bargain for Frances

1972
*Frog and Toad Together***

1984
In a Dark, Dark Room and Other Scary Stories

1986
The Josefina Story Quilt

1996
Biscuit

2005
The Berenstain Bears Clean House

2008
Fancy Nancy and the Boy from Paris

Little Critter: Snowball Soup

2010
Pinkalicious: School Rules!

2013
Pete the Cat: Pete's Big Lunch

2017
Long, Tall Lincoln

* Caldecott Honor titles
** Newbery Honor